LIMITS

PLAY SEE ASH

AF551926

GAURAV SINGH PATEL

Copyright © Gaurav Singh Patel
All Rights Reserved.

ISBN 979-888503926-0

This book has been published with all efforts taken to make the material error-free after the consent of the author. However, the author and the publisher do not assume and hereby disclaim any liability to any party for any loss, damage, or disruption caused by errors or omissions, whether such errors or omissions result from negligence, accident, or any other cause.

While every effort has been made to avoid any mistake or omission, this publication is being sold on the condition and understanding that neither the author nor the publishers or printers would be liable in any manner to any person by reason of any mistake or omission in this publication or for any action taken or omitted to be taken or advice rendered or accepted on the basis of this work. For any defect in printing or binding the publishers will be liable only to replace the defective copy by another copy of this work then available.

MY MOTHER

"SMT. USHA DEVI"

AND

MY FATHER

"MR. RAJKUMAR NIRANJAN"

Contents

Foreword *vii*

Preface *ix*

Special Thanks To *xi*

Author Introduction *xiii*

1. Play 1

2. Limit (short) 4

3. Limits 6

4. See 14

5. Lack Of 22

6. Abundance Of 26

7. Universe And God 30

8. Ash 34

My Advice 37

Foreword

This book should be read by everyone in my eyes because in this book such a situation of life has been told where we become very depressed and we feel that I have nothing in life now.

SAURABH KUMAR GAUTAM

Preface

In this book I have written some of my poems which are related to our life. Sometimes in life, despite having everything we have, we get very disappointed, on which I have written the poem "see" and another wonderful poem in my eyes "limit" which tells that there is a limit to everything in this mortal world. But there is no limit to thinking and in the end we have ended this book with a prayer of God, in which we pray to God that we should always be the same, we should never change.

GAURAV SINGH PATEL

(RESEARCHER OF ASTRONOMY PHYSICS)

Special Thanks To

Maybe I could not have reached here today without your support.

Dr. R.K. Verma

colleagues - Aman kumar yadav , Sahil kumar , Saurabh kumar gautam , Sonali srivastava , ashok yadav .

Big brothers - Premnarayn niranjan , Nikhil patel

Friends - Jitendra singh , Abhay patel.

Author Introduction

Hlo everyone my name is gaurav singh patel. I am from birpura district Jalaun U.P India. I am a mechanical Engineering student.I am 19 year old. I have been published my four research papers in astronomy physics till now and this journey is ongoing and with it i have published 4 more books on amazon till now. You can google me "Gaurav singh patel gravity" Gravity is my research topic. I can solve whole universe mystery with one concept as where is missing antimatter, how gravity work, dark matter solution, what is other side of black hole, why speed of light is constant, why gravity and time relates with each other, I can solve whole these mysterious with one concept.

In this journey i knew many things of life that i have written in this book.

Interests- astronomy physics, interference, dark matter, dark energy, time, gravity etc.

gaurav singh patel

(researcher of astronomy physics)

1. PLAY

Life plays with who is player

Luck plays with who is lucky

God plays with who is mod

Government plays with who is governor

Science plays with who is silly

Goal plays with who is coal

Service plays with who is servant

Pray plays with who is priest

School plays with who is teacher

Teacher plays with who is student

Mind plays with who is kind

Song plays with who is singer

Success plays with who is social

Dance plays with who is dancer

Art plays with who is artist

Thought plays with who is thinking

Wait plays with who is waiting

Love plays with who is lover

I plays with who is ...

2. LIMIT (Short)

On road there is speed limit

in bank there is money limit

in exam there is time limit

in physics there is unit limit

in study there is rank limit

but our think has no limit

so think beyond the limit

today universe is un limit

work hard and find its limit

this can change your status limit

and move up 1 inch than all limit

so cross the fix limit

3. LIMITS

Everything has its limit
In starting there is fundamental limit
In fundamental there is universe limit
In universe there is no galaxy limit

In galaxy there is no star limit
In star there is gravity limit
In gravity there is string hole limit
In string hole there is replace string limit

In replace string there is negative mass limit
In negative mass there is speed limit
In speed there is positive mass limit
In positive mass there is our formation limit

In our formation there is chemical limit
In babyhood there is toys limit
In child hood there is boundary limit
I an boyhood there is education limit

In education there is school limit
In road there is speed limit
In speed there is speed of lite limit
In speed there is velocity time limit

In velocity there is distance time limit
In time there is energy limit
In distance there is acceleration limit
In acceleration there is body limit

In body there is wealth limit
In wealth there is bank limit
In bank there is money limit
In money there is patient limit

In patient there is education limit
In education there is exam limit
In exam there is time limit
In time there is physics limit

In physics there is unit limit
In unit there is mks limit
In mks there is society limit
In society there is rank limit

In rank there is no future limit
In future there is excellence limit
In excellence there is matter limit
In Matter there is elastic limit

In elastic there is hooks law limit
In hooks law there is proportional limit
In proportional there is front limit
In front I have only cricket limit

In cricket there is player limit
In player there is his game limit
In game there is stregy limit
In stregy there is technical limit

In technical there is calculation limit
In calculation there is math limit
In math there is infinite limit
In infinite there is star limit

In star birth there is Chandrasekhar limit
In birth there is human limit
In human there is age limit
In age there is only number limit

In number there is distance limit
In distance there is length limit
In length there is plank limit
In plank there is hard work limit

In hard work there is study limit
In study there is night limit
In night there is society limit
In society there is job limit

In job there is family limit
In family there is age limit
In age there is short number limit
In short number there is farmer life limit

In farmer life there is rain limit
In rain there is God limit
In God there is government limit
In government there is economy limit

In economy there is gst limit
In gst there is politician limit
In politician there is boat limit
In boat there is educated human limit

In educated human there is teacher session limit
In teacher session there is student limit
In student there is discipline limit
In discipline there is character limit

In character there is books limit
In books there is words limit
In words there is meaning limit
In meaning there is learning limit

In learning there is power limit
In power there is energy limit
In energy there is mass limit
In mass there is matter limit

In matter there is molecules limit
In molecules there is atoms limit
In atoms there is fundamental limits
In fundamental that is our limit

Everything has its limit
But our think has no limit
So think beyond the limit
Today universe is unlimit

Work hard and find its limit
This can change your status limit
And move up 1 inch than all limit
So cross the limt

4. SEE

Wake up and see what is arround you

Run for health in morning

AND SEE

who runs for money in morning

Go les cabinets for fresh

AND SEE

who has no less cabinets for fresh

Take a bathe for skin

AND SEE

Who has not water for drink

Eat food for belly

AND SEE

Who has not food for live

Go for education

AND SEE

Who has no opportunity for eductation

Take tea for flavour

AND SEE

who gives you that tea

Go for lecture in classroom

AND SEE
Who sweeps that classroom

Make a loud noise

AND SEE

who is dumb

Run here to there

AND SEE

Who is lame

talk to everyone

AND SEE
Who is deep

Take a lunch

AND SEE
Who don't take breakfast till now on road

Come back after an ejoyment

AND SEE
Who work hard all over day for some money

Back to home

AND SEE
who has not home and pass whole night on road

bear different type of clothes

AND SEE

Who don't have a single type of colthes

Enjoy your evening

AND SEE

Who is wating for evening for night food

enjoy summer on beach

AND SEE

who is waiting for rain in summer

Enjoy winter

AND SEE

Who is waitng for sun lack of clothes

Enjoy rain

AND SEE
Who has not roof on his head

Enjoy color light

AND SEE
Who is waitng for a single light

Waste papers

AND SEE
Who has lack of paper for write

use branded phone

AND SEE
Who has not phone for only calling

bear branded shoe

AND SEE

who has not any type of foot wear

Sleep on bed

AND SEE
Who has not a sigle sheet for sleep

5. LACK OF

lack of water crop gets destroyed

lack of air creature gets destroyed

lack of noise meaning gets destroyed

lack of neutrons neuclius gets destroyed

lack of electrons atoms gets destroyed

lack of forces universe gets destroyed

lack of mass human gets destroyed

lack of oil vegetable gets destroyed

lack of knowledge path gets destroyed

lack of direction vector gets dstroyed

lack of sugar sweet gets destroyed

lack of milk tea gets destroyed

lack of sleep day gets destroyed

lack of light road gets destroyed

lack of salt food gets destroyed

lack of sourse talent gets destroyed

lack of money study gets destroyed

lack of timing song gets destroyed

lack of pressure volume gets destroyed

lack of service knowledge gets destroyed

lack of calm work gets destroyed

lack of source goal gets destroyed

lack of sun skin gets destroyed

lack of rain farmer gets destroyed

lack of wise life gets destroyed

lack of origin universe gets destroyed

6. ABUNDANCE OF

Abundance of water crop gets destroyed

Abundance of air creature gets destroyed

Abundance of noise meaning gets destroyed

Abundance of neutrons neuclius gets destroyed

Abundance of electrons atoms gets destroyed

Abundance of forces universe gets destroyed

Abundance of mass human gets destroyed

Abundance of oil vegetable gets destroyed

Abundance of knowledge path gets destroyed

Abundance of direction vector gets dstroyed

Abundance of sugar sweet gets destroyed

Abundance of milk tea gets destroyed

Abundance of sleep day gets destroyed

Abundance of light road gets destroyed

Abundance of salt food gets destroyed

Abundance of sourse talent gets destroyed

Abundance of money study gets destroyed

Abundance of timing song gets destroyed

Abundance of pressure volume gets destroyed

Abundance of service knowledge gets destroyed

Abundance of calm work gets destroyed

Abundance of source goal gets destroyed

Abundance of sun skin gets destroyed

Abundance of rain farmer gets destroyed

Abundance of wise life gets destroyed

Abundance of origin universe gets destroyed

7. UNIVERSE AND GOD

energy is made of string

mass is made of energy

quarks and electron is made of mass

proton and neutron made of quarks

nucleus made of proton and neutrons

atom is made of nucleus and electrons

body is made of atoms

human is made of bodies

colony is made of humans

area is made of colonies

city is made of areas

district is made of cities

state is made of district

country is made of states

continent is made of countries

planet is made of continents

solar system is made of planets

galaxy is made of solar systems

galaxy cluster is made of galaxies

supercluster is made of galaxy clusters

the universe is made of superclusters

the multiverse is made of universes

this is the made of GOD.

just made GOD defination

"GOD has not made anything

but

everything is made of GOD"

8. ASH

Till the journey of ash

we were as , we are as

we will as

this will be our face

no matter of cash

because in God face

all have same base

try to change your case.

My Advice

"It is not necessary that
you are good in every field
but there will be a field
in which you are father of all
search that"

"If you are comparing yourself with others
then you are insulting yourself
and
if you are insulting yourself then
what can other do for you imagine it
so compete with others don't compare"

"Speak little do huge
because people see more than listen
and
according to science also
speed of light is greater than sound"

"Do not believe what is your book saying
because

if books always say truth then

no one get nobel prize every year"

"There is no matter

what is your age

but this matter

think of how many age you keep"

"If any person is just smiling on your mistake

then it is more dangerous for you"

"After a hard work

when goal seems impossible

then at that time

you are very closer to your goal

so never give up

try a little more"

"Do that , that you want

but it done that he want

so

do that , that he want

definitely it done

that you want"

"It is very good to compromise
with your night
but it is very bad to compromise
with your morning"

"No work is different
but time makes it different
so every work that is done before time
is different work"

"every book is an advanture"

Printed by Libri Plureos GmbH in Hamburg,
Germany